STATE PUBL

WORTHING - LITTLEHA

RUNDEL · HENFIELD · PULBOROUGH

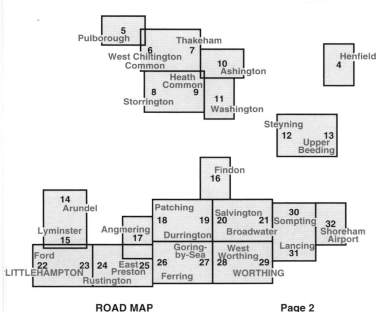

ROAD MAP — Page 2
WORTHING ENLARGED CENTRE — Page 3
INDEX TO STREETS — Page 33

Every effort has been made to verify the accuracy of information in this book but the publishers cannot accept responsibility for expense or loss caused by an error or omission. Information that will be of assistance to the user of the maps will be welcomed.

The representation on these maps of a road, track or path is no evidence of the existence of a right of way.

Car Park	🅿
Public Convenience	🅲
Place of Worship	+
One-way Street	→
Pedestrianized	▨
Post Office	●

**Scale of street plans 4 inches to 1 mile
Unless otherwise stated**

Street plans prepared and published by ESTATE PUBLICATIONS, Bridewell House, TENTERDEN, KENT, and based upon the ORDNANCE SURVEY mapping with the permission of The Controller of H. M. Stationery Office.

The Publishers acknowledge the co-operation of the local authorities of towns represented in this atlas.

Estate Publications 054 L   ISBN 0 86084 916 3   © Crown Copyright 398713

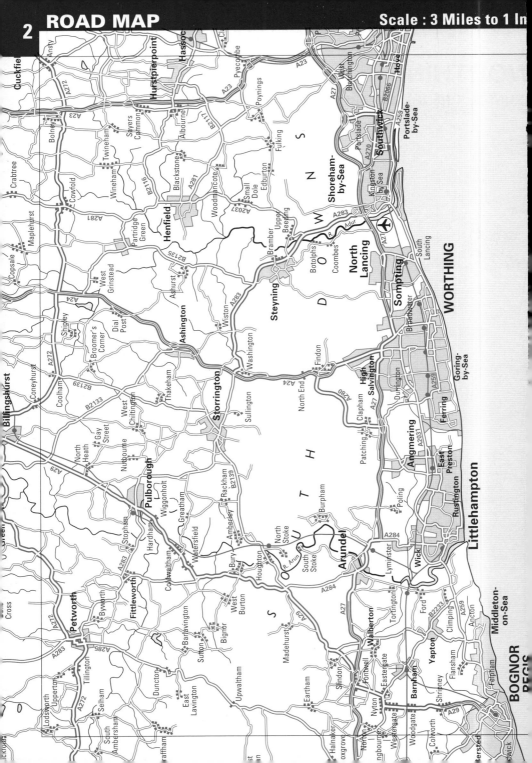

HENFIELD

4

A B C D

1

Betley Bridge

Kidders Barn

Lidde Hill Farm

A281

ALBOURNE

B2116

ROAD

CROUCH HL

Great Betley Farm

Little Betley

Parsonage Wood

Chess Bridge

Chess Brook GRN

LONDON

2

Downs Link

LANE

STONEPIT

Parsonage Farm

MALLARD WAY

STAG CL

FAWN RISE

DEER

ST PETERS WY

PARK WAY

MAID-MENT CT

Sewage Works

WANTLEY HILL ESTATE

Medical Centre

ROAD

LONDON

MANOR WAY

MANOR CL

3

STONEPIT

STAPLES PL

STAPLES BARN

GRESHAM PL

FABIANS

KINGSFIELD

NORTHCROFT

C of E School

Cemy

Leisure Centre

Rec Grnd

FARM CL

ROCKETS CL

PARSONAGE

CHANTRY CL

MARTYN CL

THE LAURELS

BENSON RD

NYES CL

FURNERS

ROAD

Henfield

DOWNS VW TER

STAPLES BARN

FLOWER FARM

NORTH CROFT CL

Pot Sta

LANE

UPPER

GREEN WAYS

STATION

BROOMFIELD

ROAD

NORTH ROAD

CHURCH

CHURCH TER

CHEST NUT WY

NUT WY

BRO

CHU LA

HOG TAN LA

THE STREET

BISHOP LA

COOPERS

FURNERS MEAD

FURNERS WY

THE DAISYCROFT

MEAD

4

WEST

LANE END

LAWYERS LANE

Nursery

Dears Farm

HOLLANDS

STATION RD

BEECHINGS

LOWER

GANDERS

FAIRCOX

LOWER FAIRCOX

BATTS DR

KNOWLES

CL

BROWNINGS

CHU TAN

Library

WOOLVENS ROW

Oratory

LOVERS WK

PARK RD

CAGEFOOT LA

Hall

STIPENHOKE

HIGH ST

Henfield Comm

LOWER STATION ROAD

DROPPING HOLMS

CROFT LA

CHANCTONBURY VW

MILL ROAD

THE HOOKS

BLACKGATE LA

HEWITTS CL

END

HEWITTS RD

GOLDEN SQ

Fire Sta

BRIGHTON

CEDAR

MILL DR

Sch

ROAD

West End

HOLLANDS

BUCKWISH LA

5

Buckwish Farm

SANDY LANE

Little Barn

WINDMILL LANE

NEP LANE

KING JAMES LANE

SOUTH VW

TER

Nep Town

GRINSTEAD

Rec Grnd

TOWN

WEA

NEW

Spring Hill

BARROW

HILL

LANE

Barrowhill Farm

Broadmare Farm

RO

A2

The Rye

Rye Farm

DAGBROOK

Broadmare Common

Nightingal Hall

6

Brookside Farm

BARN

LANE

New Barn Farm

NEW

A B C D

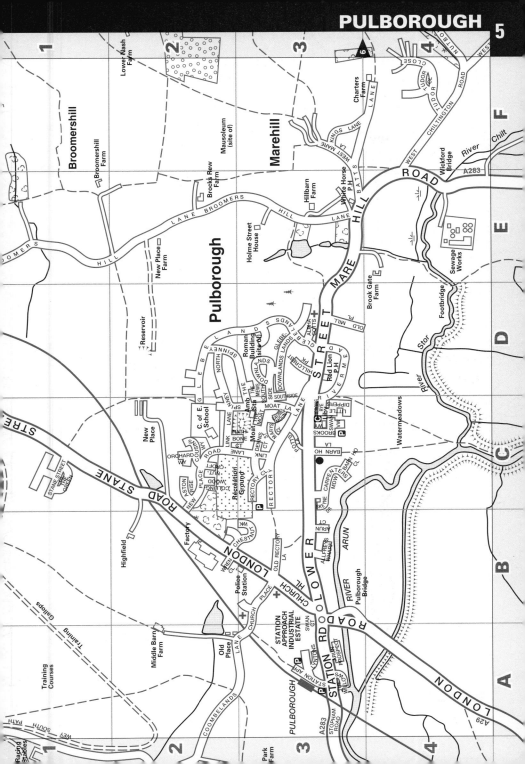

Broomershill

Marehill

Pulborough

Lower Nash Farm

Broomershill Farm

Mausoleum (site of)

Brooks Rew Farm

Charters Farm

White Horse

Hillbarn Farm

WEST MARE KINGS LANE

WEST CHILLTINGTON ROAD

NUTBO... WEST

CLOSE

TUDOR CT

TUDOR ROAD

Wickford Bridge

River Chilt

A283

ROAD

WEST HILL

MARE STREET

HILL BATTS LANE

New Place Farm

Reservoir

Holme Street House

BROOMERS HILL LANE

Roman Building (site of)

Brook Gate Farm

Sewage Works

STANE STREET

COOMBELANDS

LONDON ROAD

STANE ROAD

New Place

C. of E. School

GLEBELANDS NORTH

SPINNEY

THE MEWS

LINK LANE

SWAN LANE

ORCHARD CT

ASTON

NEW PLACE RISE

Recreation Ground

OLD PLACE

SPINNEY SIDE

DOWNLANDS SOUTH

GLEBELANDS SOUTH

MOAT CT

BONE CT

BATH PL

MOAT LANE

DENNS CT

STARYS

RECTORY CL

RECTORY LANE

POTTS LANE

LINK LANE

Red Lion P.H.

DOWNLANDS SIDE

SOUTHSIDE

GLEBE RD

HILLCREST PK

AYLING PL

OLD MILL PL

STREET

VERMEN

DIPPERS

BROOKS

BARN HO

SWAN HO...

CARPEN...

MOW BARN CL

NEW BARN CL

LA

Watermeadows

River Stor

Stor

Footbridge

River Arun

LOWER STREET

Highfield

Factory

Police Station

CHESTNUT

WREN CT

OLD RECTORY LA

CHURCH PLACE

CHURCH HL

SWAN CT

STATION APPROACH INDUSTRIAL ESTATE

LONDON ROAD

ARUN CL

ALLFREYS WHARF

STATION RD

STATION APP

KITTONS PROSPECT

RIVER ARUN

Pulborough Bridge

Middle Barn Farm

Old Place

CHURCH LANE

PULBOROUGH

A283

STOPHAM ROAD

LONDON ROAD A29

Racing Stables

Training Gallops

WAY SOUTH PATH

Training Courses

Park Farm

1   2   3   4

F

E

D

C

B

A

1   2   3   4

6

A **B** **C** **D**

1

5

2

3

4

5

6

Nutbourne Place Farm

Shorts Farm

Vineyard

Golf Course

Club House

Huntl Fruit F

Nutbourne

Marsh Farm

Nursery

West Chiltington

DELL

ORCHARD

Dennis Marcus Farm

BROAD

Kings and Princes Farm

HOLLOW STREET

CHURCH STREET

Museum

NUTBOURNE LA

THE STREET

NUTBOURNE ROAD

STREAM

ROAD

Mill Farm

Stream Farm

STREET GAY

LANE GAY

STREAM LANE

Meers Farm

Churchfield Farm

CURBEY CL

HOLLY CLOSE

LANE THE

Recreation Ground

Hall

Nutbourne Common

ROAD

WEST CHILTINGTON ROAD

Heath Mill

Nursery

HARBOROUGH MDW

HARBOROUGH GORSE

NEW BARN LANE

HARBOROUGH DR

HARBOROUGH HILL

HARBOROUGH

MONKMEAD

CASTLEGATE

Finches

FINCHES

FOXFIELDS

THE COMMON

LITTLE

HILL

MILL HILL

MILL LANE

West Chiltington Common

MARTLETS

MILL END

DARK LANE

BIRCH END

LARCH END

COPSE

HAGLANDS

River Chilt

River

Silver WOOD

SILVER WOOD

KINGS-WOOD

NYETIMBER COPSE

SILVER LANE

MONKMEAD LANE

NYETIMBER

HEATHFIELD COPSE

BARKWORTH WY

THE BIRCHES

Police Ho

MORRIS WY

HAGLANDS

COMMON ROAD

CHESTNUTTLES

RIDGE

NIGHTINGALLES

LANE

HINDLE

HAGLANDS

LORDINGS

Smo Alle

Hurston Warren

Golf

Course

Club House

NYETIMBER COPSE

BROOK CHASE

Fish Pond

RAMBLEDOWN LA

CHILTINGTON CL

CROSSWAYS

GARDEN WOOD CL

CROSSWAYS

PK

WILLOW CL

BIRCH TRE

SILVER GLAD

MONKMEAD LANE

WESTWARD LANE

MONKMEAD

WYNDHAM LEA

COMMON HILL

FIR TREE

FIR TREE LANE

BIRCH GRO

BADGERS WOOD

BOWER

GROVE

ROUNDABOUT COPSE

HEATHER LANE

SUNSET LANE

SUNSET LANE

SPINNEY LA

BIRCH LANE

HILL

ROUNDABOUT

Threals Copse

Roundabout Farm

River Stor

Hurston Place Farm

Hurston Place

HURSTON LA

SPINNEY

Perretts Copse

WEST CHILTINGTON

GREENHURST LA

RB

A **B** **8** **C** **D**

E | F | G | H

Knowe Top

Park Barn

B2139

ROAD

PICKETTS COTTAGES

Laybrook Farm

B2133

1

Oakwood Farm

atchs arm

Lower Voakes Farm

CHILLINGTON

Goffsland House

Nurseries

Homelea Farm

STREET WEST

Nursery

Fly Farm

LANE

SINNOCKS LANE

COOLHAM ROAD

ROAD

Lower Crays Farm

2

Upper Crays Farm

Southlands Farm

DUKES

HILL

Town House Farm

CRAYS LANE

3

ry

DS

THE STREET

BRAMBLE LANE

Reservoir

Sch

+

Sewage Wks

ROAD

WOODLAND COTTAGES

Thakeham

4

umping Station

Chesswood Nursery

Village Hall
Rec Grnd

St Marys Well

10

Nurseries

Rec Grnd

BAR

HIGH

HAZEL

BARN

LANE

TROTS

Thakeham Place Farm

LANE

5

Highbar Copse

COPSE

LINFIELD

GUYHURS SPINNEY

FURZE COMMON RD

Abingworth

Ma E

Champions Farm

JACKETS

STORRINGTON

HILL

Nursery

STRAWBERRY LANE

Threals Farm

B2139

Green Dene Farm

RAWBERRY LANE

Guyhurst Copse

6

E | F | G | H

9

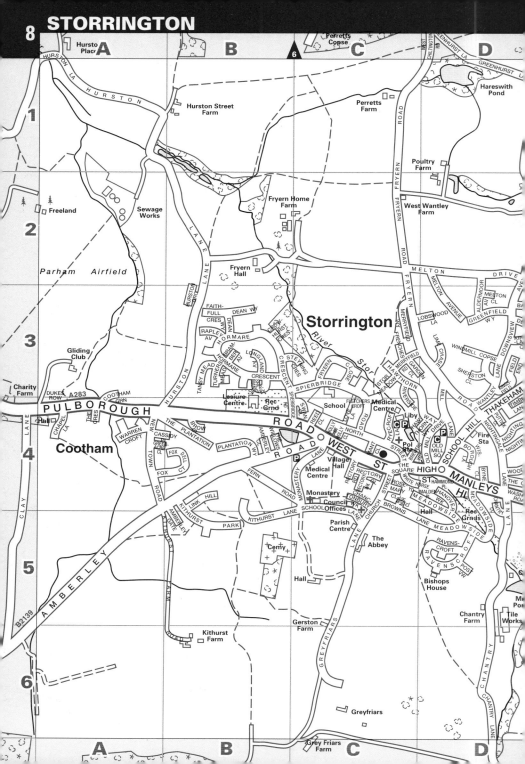

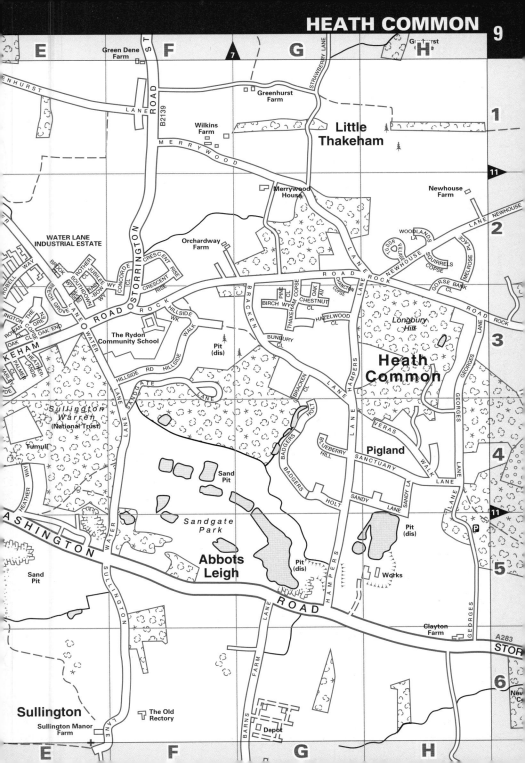

E **F** **G** **H**

Green Dene Farm

Greenhurst Farm

B2139

MERRYWOOD

Wilkins Farm

Merrywood House

Little Thakeham

Newhouse Farm

WATER LANE INDUSTRIAL ESTATE

Orchardway Farm

WOODLANDS LA.

TUDOR WILLOW

SQUIRRELS COPSE

MELROSE PL

GORSE BANK CL

STORRINGTON ROAD

CRESCENT RISE

CRESCENT RISE

ROCK

HILLSIDE WK

HILLSIDE WALK

The Rydon Community School

BRACKEN

PINE CL

BIRCH WY

THAKEHAM COPSE

CHINCTON COPSE

OAK AV

CHESTNUT CL

HAZELWOOD CL

BUNBURY CL

Pit (dis)

Longbury Hill

Heath Common

NEWHOUSE

ROCK ROAD

ROAD

GEORGES

KEHAM

OAK

CLSE

OAK END

THE GREY

ROWAN COPSE

HEATHER

PALMER

SANDS

HILLSIDE RD

HILLSIDE

SANDGATE LANE

BRACKEN CL

LANE

HAMPERS LANE

HOLT

BADGERS

BLUEBERRY HILL

VERAS

SANCTUARY

Pigland

WALK

GEORGES LANE

Sullington Warren (National Trust)

Tumuli

WATER

LANE

Sand Pit

Sandgate Park

BADGERS HOLT

SANDY LANE

SANDY LA

LANE

11

P

HEATHER WAY

Abbots Leigh

Pit (dis)

HAMPERS LANE

Pit (dis)

Works

5

Sand Pit

ASHINGTON

SULLINGTON

ROAD

FARM LANE

Clayton Farm

GEORGES

A283 STOR

Sullington

Sullington Manor Farm

The Old Rectory

BARNS FARM LANE

Depot

New Co

6

1
2
3
4
5
6

11

E **F** **G** **H**

Calves Wood
Hooklands
A24
Brickyard Farm
Hook Farm
Belchins Wood
Brownhill Wood
East Wolves Farm
America Wood
Broadbridge Farm
Sewage Works
Kensetts Corner
HOLE
Spear Hill
Nursery
Holmbush House
Martins Farm
HOOKLANDS LANE
BILLINGSHURST ROAD
B2133
Westlands Farm
Westlands Farm
West Wolves Farm
Oast House Farm
IVY LA
GREEN ACRES
ALICIA AV
RECTORY
WIND MILL
THE CLOSE
HILLCREST
WEST
HILLCREST DRIVE
DRIVE
AREA
LONDON
MOR LEYS
FAIRFIELD RD
SMITHS
BLACKSMITHS
MILL MEAD
WILLOW WAY
BROOK SIDE
LONDON ROAD
LANE
Ashington
THE Sch
SANDS
Melros Farm
WARM-INGHURST CL
MEIROS WAY
Nursery
PENN GDNS
Brook
Lancing
CHURCH
Church Farm
MILL LANE
FAIRFIELD RD
Moat
New Barn
Warminghurst Farm
Warminghurst
RECTORY LANE
PARK
Mill Copse
St Marys Well
Manor House Buildings
PARK LANE
LANE
Park Barn
Jinkes Farm
Newhouse Farm

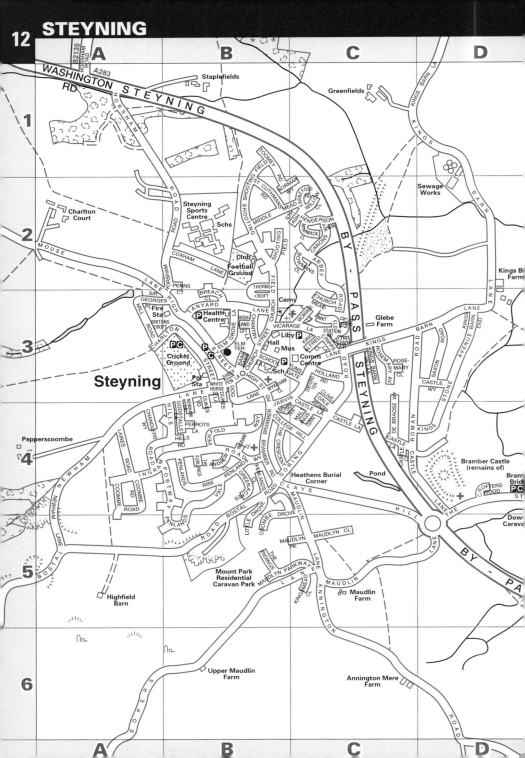

Steyning

Horton
Wood

Clay
Pit

Tip
(dis)

Nightingales

A2037

RIVER ADUR

Saltworks

Freeland
Cottages

Horton
Hall

HENFIELD ROAD

Works

Upper Horton
Farm

The
Priory

Caravan
Site

THE PADDOCKS

THE DRIFTWAY

PEPPERSCOMBE LA

DEACONS

Pound
House
Farm

BRIDLE CL

SMUGGLERS LA

Caravan
Site

CHURCH

PRIORY

CHURCH LANE

ST PETERS

THORNS

SCHOOL

MONKS ROAD

WAY

GRN

THE

FIELD

Caravan
Site

CL

THORNS

Sch

Rec.
Grnd.

Sports
Centre

SALTINGS

CHURCH

WAY

HYDE

STREET

HYDE SQ

UNDERMILL LANE

POUND

DOWNLAND
RD

TRULEIGH

WIND-
MILL
CL

TOWERS

NEWLAND ROAD

ADUR VALLEY
COLLEGE

MANOR ROAD

RD

Windmill   Hill

Golding Barn
Farm

STREET HIGH

Beeding
Bridge

ADUR

DAWN

Hall

DAWN CL

CRESCENT

SELE GDNS

THE

NEW RD

FLORETS

STREET

DOWNS

TWITTEN

HOBS
ACRE

MAINES ROAD

MANOR ROAD

THE

**Upper
Beeding**

Bramber

Rising Sun
P.H

Convent

HENFIELD

Beeding
Court
Farm

New House
Farm

**Castle
Town**

Cultivation
Terraces

TEYNING

Saltworks

BY - PASS

SHOREHAM ROAD

A2283
SHOREHAM ROAD

BOSTEL

nnington
Farm

5
6
7
8 D1

Nurseries

Brook
Lawn

Brookfield

Wick
F.C

GRANGE

Rec

MINSTER ROAD

HEAD RD

FIELD RD

LANE

COOMBES WAY

CRES

CRES

GRIFFIN

Wick

Broomhurst
Farm

ROAD

Lyminster

Camp
Site

WOODCOTE LA

Caravan
Park

FULLERS

MILL CREEK

SANDFIELD AV

SEATON

SEATON

SEATON

LYMINSTER RD 284

NORTHAM

F

LYMINSTER

Knucker
Hole

CHURCH LA

THE PADDOCK

LYMINSTER

ROAD

MEAD ROAD

OLD

Nurseries

CHA

EAGLE

SANDFIELD

AV

KESTREL

KESTREL

GDNS

CRES

FINCHES

COURTWICK

LANE

NEW

COURT

MARTELLO
ENTERPRISE PARK

E

Church
Farm

Brookside
Caravan Park

Thornden
Caravan Park

FALCON

GLD EDWARDS

ROBIN WAY

SWIFT

23

Ditch

Black

COURTWICK

Court Wick
Park

Nursery

D

Watermeadows

Brook Barn
Farm

Littlehampton
Junction

C

Watermeadows

Arundel
Junction

22

B

RIVER ARUN

Watermeadows

A

Tortington

FORD ROAD

Manor
Farm

College

The Equine
Veterinary Hospital

Arundel
Arms P.H

THE WILLOWS

GAUGEMASTER

FORD

STATION ROAD

Camping
Site

Marina

FORD

New
Barn

5
6
7
8

FORD
ROI

A B C D

North End

Pest Ho

Broad Wood

1

Ramsdean Plantation

Crematorium

Keepers Plantation

Gallops Farm

2

Kings Wood

Coventry Plantation

Tumuli

HORSHAM ROAD A24

Fire Sta

NIGHTINGALES
THE OVAL
THE BARN
HIGHBARN
HIGH BARN

Findon

The Downs (Training Stables)

The Gibbet

A280

LONG FURLONG

The Kennels

DOWNVIEW RD
BEECH
BEECH
LIME
ASH RD
ELM RISE
KILMORE CL
LANE
ARCH
PONY FARM

Tumili

3

SCHOOL HILL
HOMEWOOD
HORSHAM ROAD
NEPCOTE CROSS
THE WILLOWS
STABLE LANE

New Forest

Sch
Cemy
Hall

North Park

Home of the Holy Rood (Convent)

SUMMER FIELDS
WESTVIEW PADDOCK

North Park Gate

HERMIT TER

HOLMCROFT GDNS
SOUTH VW RD
NORTHVIEW TER

LANE

Nepcote Lodge

Nepcote Green

Park

The Paddock

St John The Baptists

Findon Place

STEEP

Findon Tower

STEEP CL

CONVENT

FOX LEY
NEPFIELD CL

✛ **Nepcote**

4

Church Hill

South Park

Flint Mines

HIGH STREET
BY PASS
FINDON

THE CHASE
THE CHASE

NEPCOTE LANE

Cissbury

Cissbury Farm

5

Church Hill Shaw

Birch Plantation

ROGERS LANE

Nurseries

THE QUADRANGLE
THE

FINDON BY PASS

Hill Barn Covert

Rogers Farm

New Plantation

The Vale

6

The Oaks

West Hill

GALLOPS
THE HILL
DOWNSIDE AV
DOWNSIDE CL
DOWNSIDE AVENUE

P

MAY TREE
STORRINGTON RISE
SULLINGTON GARDENS
LONG MEADOW

P

ROAD A24

HAZELHURST CRES

AVENUE

CENTRAL AVENUE

CISS

HOLL

A B 20 C D

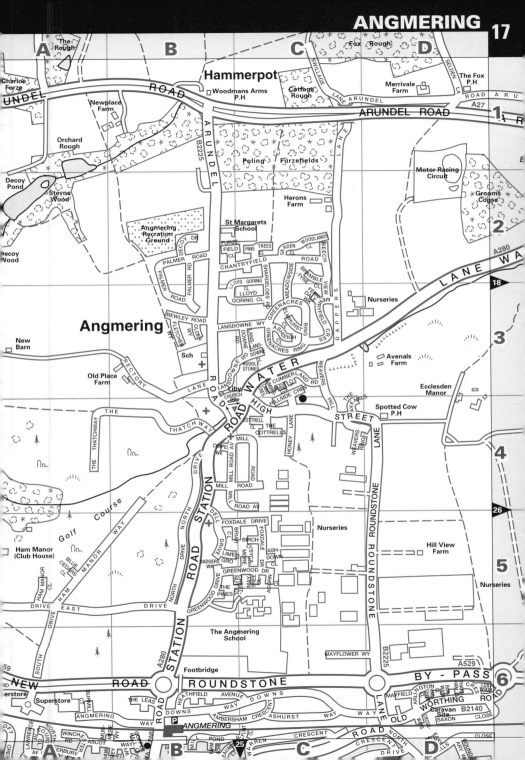

Hammerpot

Angmering

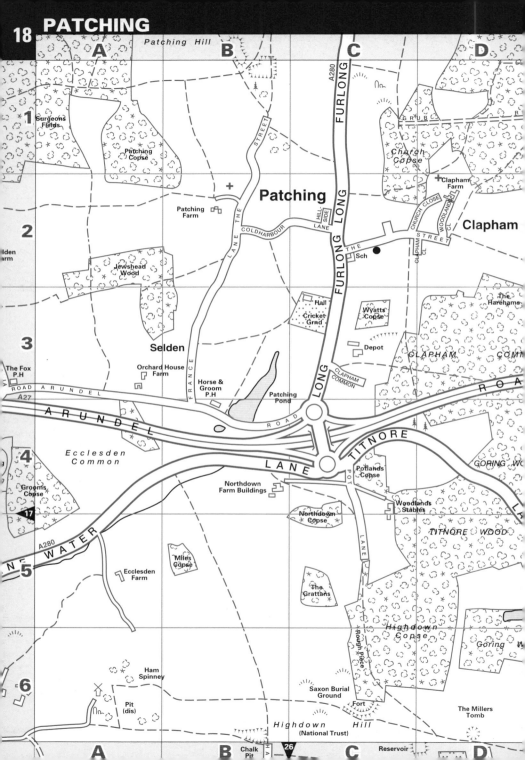

A   **B**   **C**   **D**

Patching Hill

Surgeons Fields

Patching Copse

A280 FURLONG

GRUB

Church Copse

R

Clapham Farm

Patching Farm

THE LANE

COLDHARBOUR

Patching

HILL-SIDE LANE

FURLONG LONG

CHURCH CLOSE

WOODLANDS CL

Clapham

STREET

Patching

lden arm

Jewshead Wood

FRANCE LANE

THE Sch

CLAPHAM STREET

Wyatts Copse

The Harehams

Hall

Cricket Grnd

Selden

Orchard House Farm

Horse & Groom P.H

Depot

CLAPHAM COMMON

CLAPHAM COMM

The Fox P.H

ROAD   ARUNDEL

A27

Patching Pond

LONG

CLAPHAM COMMON

ROA

Patching Pond

Ecclesden Common

ARUNDEL

LANE

ROAD

TITNORE

GORING WO

Grooms Copse

17

Northdown Farm Buildings

Potlands Copse

Woodlands Stables

LA

NE   WATER

A280

Northdown Copse

POT LANE

TITNORE WOOD

Miles Copse

Ecclesden Farm

The Grattans

Highdown Copse

Goring W

Ham Spinney

Rough Piece

Saxon Burial Ground

Fort

The Millers Tomb

Pit (dis)

Highdown Hill
(National Trust)

A   **B**   Chalk Pit   **26**   **C**   Reservoir   **D**

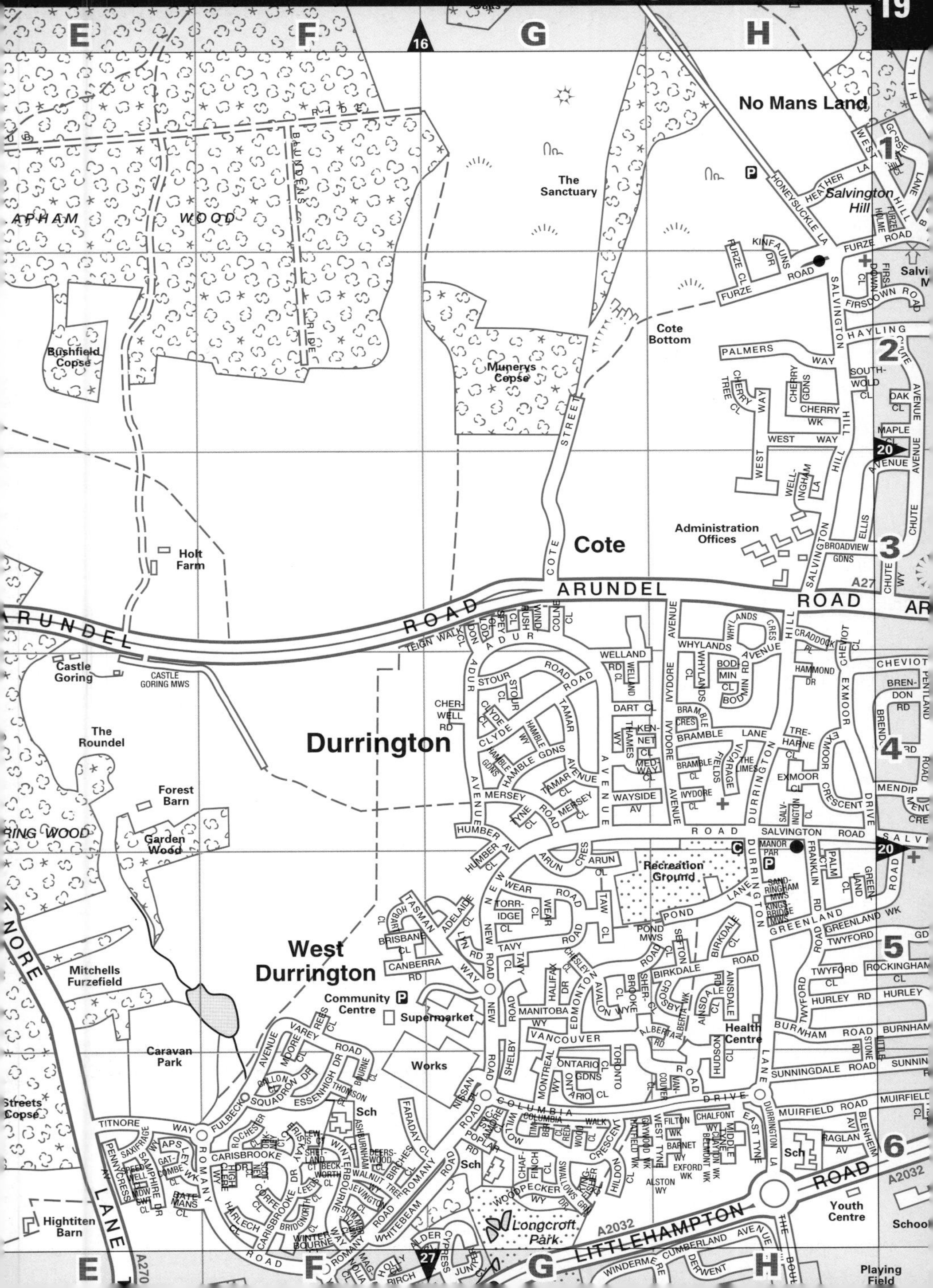
E
F
G
H
16
27
20
1
2
3
4
5
6
No Mans Land
Salvington Hill
The Sanctuary
Cote Bottom
Munerys Copse
Bushfield Copse
APHAM WOOD
BLUNDENS RIDE
RIDE
Holt Farm
Cote
Administration Offices
COTE STREET
ARUNDEL ROAD
A27
Castle Goring
CASTLE GORING MWS
The Roundel
Forest Barn
RING WOOD
Garden Wood
Durrington
West Durrington
Mitchells Furzefield
Caravan Park
Streets Copse
Hightiten Barn
TITNORE LANE
TITNORE WAY
A270
Community Centre
Supermarket
Works
Sch
Recreation Ground
Health Centre
Youth Centre
School
Playing Field
Longcroft Park
LITTLEHAMPTON ROAD
A2032
COLUMBIA DRIVE
SALVINGTON ROAD
DURRINGTON LANE
DURRINGTON HILL
SALVINGTON HILL
WEST WAY
PALMERS WAY
CHERRY TREE CL
CHERRY GDNS
CHERRY WK
WELLINGHAM LA
FURZE ROAD
FURZE CL
KINFAUNS DR
HONEYSUCKLE LA
HEATHER LA
WEST HILL
GORSE AV
FIRSDOWN ROAD
HAYLING
SOUTHWOLD CL
OAK CL
MAPLE AVENUE
CHUTE AVENUE
CHUTE WAY
ELLIS
BROADVIEW GDNS
WHYLANDS AVENUE
WHYLANDS CL
WHYLANDS CRES
CRADDOCK PL
CHEVIOT CL
CHEVIOT
HAMMOND DR
BODMIN RD
BODMIN CL
IVYDORE AVENUE
IVYDORE CL
BRAMBLE LANE
BRAMBLE CRES
BRAMBLE CL
VICARAGE FIELDS
THE LIMES
TREHARNE CL
EXMOOR DRIVE
EXMOOR CRESCENT
EXMOOR CL
BRENDON RD
PENTLAND
MENDIP
SALVINGTON CL
FRANKLIN RD
PALM CT
GREEN LAND CL
GREENLAND ROAD
GREENLAND WK
MANOR PAR
SANDRINGHAM MWS
KINGSBRIDGE MWS
TWYFORD ROAD
TWYFORD CL
ROCKINGHAM CL
HURLEY RD
BURNHAM ROAD
STONE RD
SUNNINGDALE ROAD
MUIRFIELD ROAD
RAGLAN AV
BLENHEIM AV
TEIGN WALK
SPEY CL
DON CL
ADUR AVENUE
ADUR CL
WINDRUSH CL
COLNE CL
STOUR ROAD
STOUR CL
TAMAR ROAD
TAMAR AVENUE
TAMAR CL
CHERWELL RD
CLYDE CL
CLYDE RD
HAMBLE WY
HAMBLE GDNS
WELLAND RD
WELLAND CL
DART CL
THAMES WY
KENNET CL
MEDWAY CL
WAYSIDE AV
MERSEY RD
MERSEY CL
TYNE CL
HUMBER AV
HUMBER CL
ARUN CRES
ARUN CL
NEW ROAD
WEAR ROAD
WEAR CL
TORRIDGE CL
TAW CL
POND LANE
POND MWS
TASMAN WAY
HOBART CL
ADELAIDE CL
BRISBANE CL
CANBERRA RD
LYN RD
TAVY CL
TAVY RD
SETON RD
BIRKDALE ROAD
BIRKDALE CL
AINSDALE RD
AINSDALE CL
CROSBY CL
SHERCL
BROOKE CL
AVALON WY
CHESLEY
EDMONTON RD
HALIFAX DR
MANITOBA WY
VANCOUVER ROAD
ALBERTA WK
ALBERTA RD
HUDSON CL
ONTARIO CL
ONTARIO GDNS
TORONTO CL
MONTREAL AV
SHELBY RD
VANCOUVER CL
NISSAN PL
SYCAMORE CL
WILLOW CRESCENT
COLUMBIA WALK
POPLAR
FINCH CL
CHAFFINCH CL
SWALLOWS GRN
WOODPECKER WY
KINGFISHER
HILDON CL
GAYWOOD WK
HATFIELD WK
WEST TYNE
FILTON WK
BARNET WY
EXFORD WK
ALSTON WY
CHALFONT WY
CLAYTON WK
BELMONT WK
MIDDLE TYNE
EAST TYNE
VAREY RD
REES CL
MOORE CL
CALLON CL
SQUADRON DR
ESSENHIGH DR
THOMSON
BOURNE CL
FULBECK AV
ROMANY ROAD
FARADAY CL
ROCHESTER
CARISBROOKE DR
HIGH CLERE WY
ERISKAY CT
LEWIS CT
SHETLAND CT
BECKWORTH CL
WINTERBOURNE WAY
ASHBURNHAM CL
DEERSWOOD CL
WALNUT TREE
BIRCHES
ROMANY
SAXIFRAGE
PENNYCRESS AV
SPEEDWELL
SAMPHIRE DR
GATCOMBE CL
BATEMANS CL
HARLECH CL
CORFE CL
LEEDS CL
BRIDGNORTH CL
JEVINGTON CL
WHITEBEAM RD
ALDER CL
CYPRESS
JUNIPER CL
HOLLY CL
BIRCH
MAGNOLIA CL
WINDERMERE
DERWENT
CUMBERLAND AVENUE
THE BOULEVARD

E F G H

Beggers Bush

Lychpole Hill

1

Bottom

Tenants Hill

Titch Hill Farm

2

Coombe Barn

Lambleys Barn

The Mountain

30

THE NORE

Quarry (dis)

Sompting Abbotts

3

Church Farm

School

Playing Field

A27

LANE FIRST AV LONGLANDS GLADE LONGLANDS SPINNEY FIRST LONGLANDS

Football Grnd

DOWNLANDS BUSINESS PARK

TITCH HILL CHURCH LANE TITCH HILL LANE

FOURTH AVENUE CHARMANWAY LYONS

DOWNLANDS RETAIL PARK

BY - PASS

4

Recreation Ground

Superstore

LYONS SOMPTING LANE

Nursery

B2222

30

THIRD AVENUE BEECHES AVENUE PINES AVENUE LYONS WAY WAY

WEST STREET

LORYS Co

SECOND AVENUE LYONS WAY

ROAD

UPPER BRIGHTON ROAD

NERMANS GDNS

TRISTRAM CL

C

PER BRIGHTON ROAD SOMPTING AVENUE

TEMPLARS BOROUGH MORLAND RD TURNER AV BRAMBER AV ALLING

Broadwater

FEVERIL CL LOOSE LANE RIL

5

Masonic Hall CHARMANDEAN LANE

DOWNLANDS GDNS LEIGHTON AV GAINS TON RD

DOWNLANDS PARK HADLEY SHANDON LANE HAW THORN GDNS FOREST ROAD BRAMLEY WY BRA EHAN DON WY

PAK-MEAD CRES SOUTHWAYS Sch ROAD

Lyons Farm Rec Grnd

CLARENDON

CISSBURY ROAD HAWTHORN RD HAWTHORN CRES HIGHL RD SAND

LEIGH ROAD BRAMLEY SO BI SIO MWS BINGHAM

CHARMANDEAN ROAD

SLINDON BLINTON

KINGSLAND

BROADWATER WAY

SOUTHFIELD ROAD

FOREST ROAD WIGMORE ROAD BRAMLEY ROAD SOMPTING ROAD NORTHBROOK ROAD

NORTHBROOK TRADING ESTATE

SOUTHDOWN VIEW E SOUTHDOWN VIEW W SOUTHDOWN VIEW WEST

BROADWATER TRADING ESTATE

Sports Ground

6

CROCKERS PARADE P BROADWATER STREET WEST URCHENS RY Sch CARNEGIE ROAD College

BROADWATER GARDENS BROADWATER STREET EAST PENFOLD ROAD

School

DOMINION WY WEST

DOMINION WY EASTING

SOMPTING BR E AVENUE

MANOR RD BEAUMONT RD CHASE MARLOWE RD FLETCHER RD

DOMINION RD

School Liby

DOWNVIEW HAMILTON RD HARRISON ROAD HARRISON ROAD SOUTH DOWNVIEW RUSSELL RD DECOY WY DEACON WY DOM

EAST WORTHING TRADING ESTATE

Manor Sports Ground

29

B2223

E F G H

A B C D

Works

Lower
Farm

FORD LANE

Works

Ford

1

RODNEY CRESCENT

NELSON ROW

FORD LANE

15

Littlehampton
Junction

RIVER ARUN

2

*Ford
Aerodrome
(disused)*

H.M
Prison

H.M
Prison

Sewage
Works

RUDFORD
INDUSTRIAL ESTATE

3

ROAD

LANE

CHURCH

Church
Farm

GREEN

LANE

Nursery

B2233

HORSEMERE

APPLE TREE WK

APPLE
TREE WK

Caravan
Park

Climping

Caravan
Park

RD

4

YAPTON

**Horsemere
Green**

LANE

Hall

LANE BRIDGE

FERRY

R

CROOKTHORN

CROOKTHORN

BROOKPIT LANE

ROAD

LANE CROOKTHORN

CLIMPING

LANGMEAD CL

Hobbs
Farm

Sch

LANE

Brookpits
Manor

Kents
Farm

Rye bank Rife

Ryebank

A259

GREVATTS

5

Hobbs
New Barn

Rye Bank
Buildings

Sewage
Works

The Bank House
P.H

New
Barn

6

STREET

Moat

Hotel

Atherington

A B C D

P

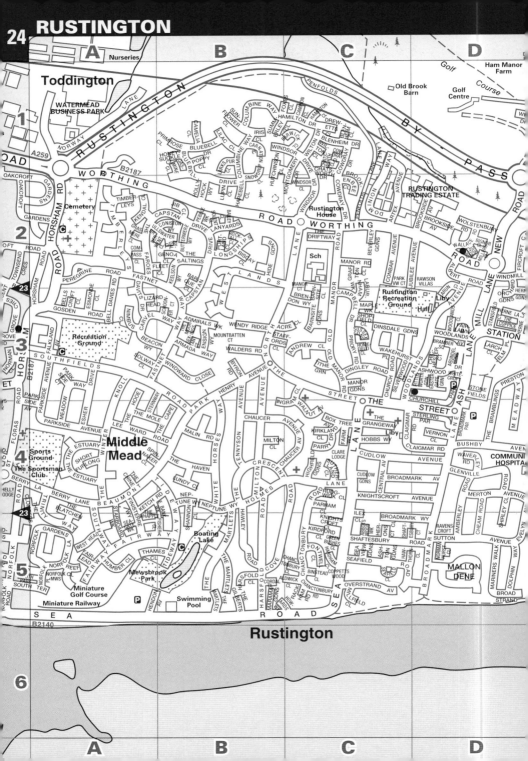

Rustington

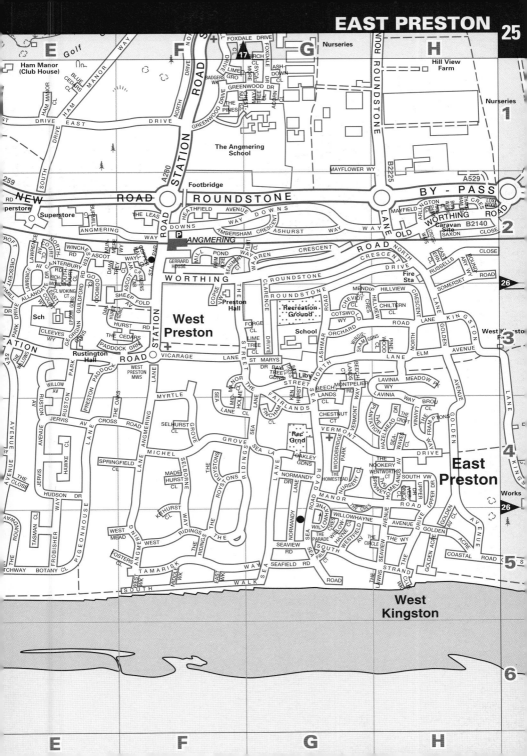

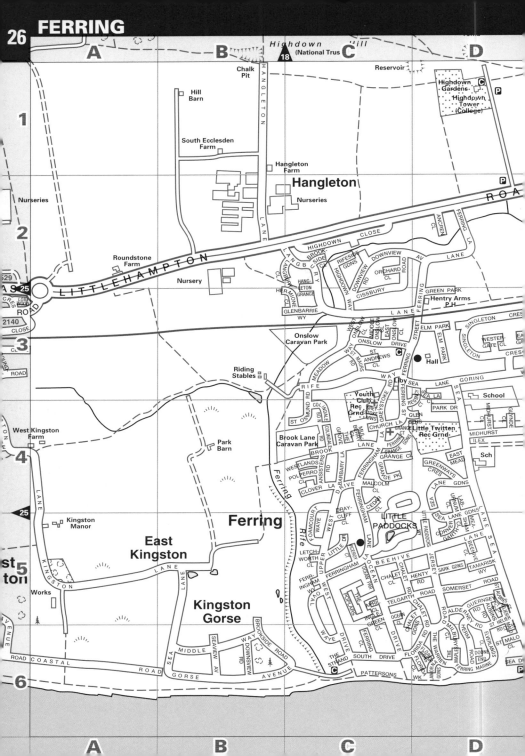

West Tarring

West Worthing

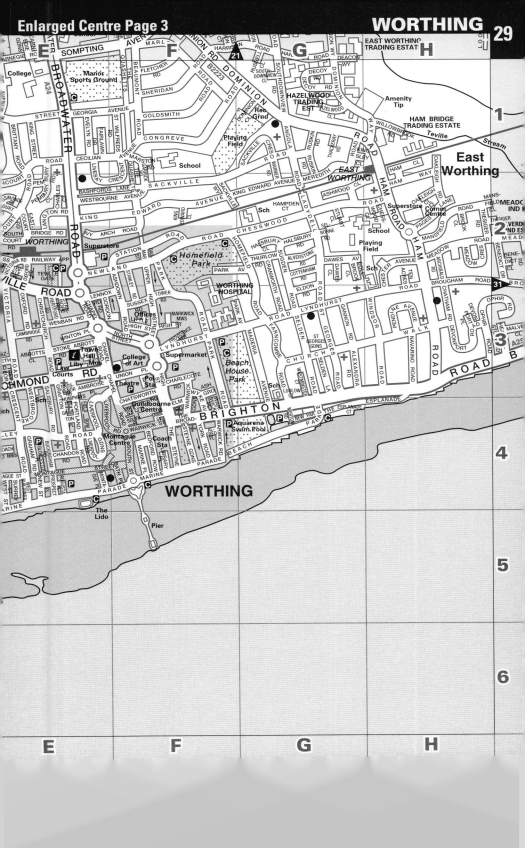

WORTHING

East Worthing

BRIGHTON

Notable locations marked on the map:
- College
- Manor Sports Ground
- Playing Field
- School
- EAST WORTHING TRADING ESTATE
- HAZELWOOD TRADING EST
- Amenity Tip
- HAM BRIDGE TRADING ESTATE
- Teville Stream
- Superstore
- Comm Centre
- Playing Field
- Rec Grnd
- Homefield Park
- WORTHING HOSPITAL
- Offices
- Town Hall
- Liby Mus
- College of Art
- Law Courts
- Theatre
- Police Sta
- Supermarket
- Beach House Park
- Guildbourne Centre
- Montague Centre
- Coach Sta
- Library
- Aquarena Swim. Pool
- The Lido
- Pier

Grid references: E, F, G, H (top and bottom); 1, 2, 3, 4, 5, 6 (right side)

Road junction numbers: 21, 31

Selected street names visible:
SOMPTING, BROADWATER, DOMINION RD, AVENUE, SHERIDAN RD, FLETCHER RD, BEAUMONT, GOLDSMITH, GEORGIA AVENUE, EVELYN RD, FAIRLAWN, ST WILFREDS, CONGREVE, CECILIAN, LIVESEY, MARSTON GDNS, GARRICK, SACKVILLE, BASHFORDS LANE, WESTBOURNE AVENUE, KING EDWARD AVENUE, IVY ARCH ROAD, CHESSWOOD ROAD, KING STREET, PEMBURY, CHARLES, STATION, CAMBRIDGE RD, WINTON PL, STOKE ABBOTT, NORTH STREET, HIGH STREET, UNION, CHAPEL RD, LYNDHURST, CHATSWORTH, WARWICK, MARINE PARADE, THE STEYNE, YORK RD, BEDFORD, STEYNE GDNS, MARINE PLACE, THE ESPLANADE, BRIGHTON ROAD, HAM ROAD, WINDSOR ROAD, NAVARINO ROAD, ALEXANDRA ROAD, DEVONPORT, OPHIR, RICHMOND RD, MONTAGUE STREET, LIVERPOOL RD, SALISBURY, GRAFTON, GRATWICKE, CHANDOS RD, VICTORIA RD

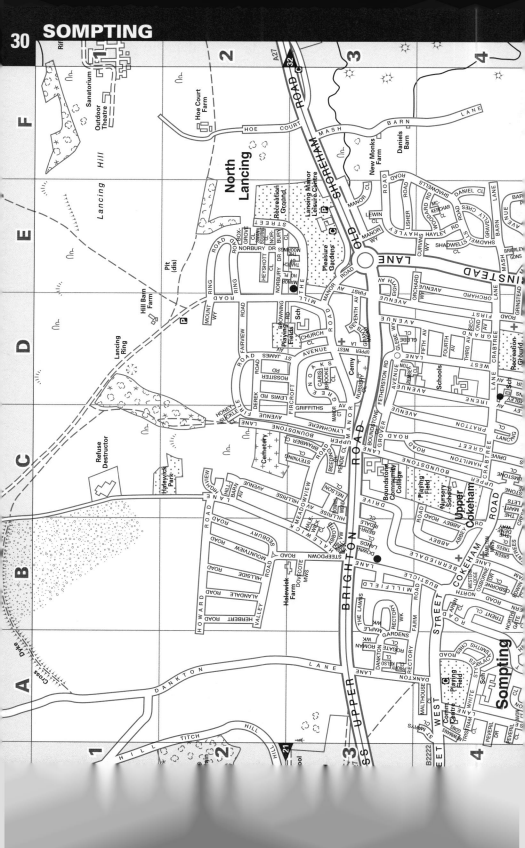

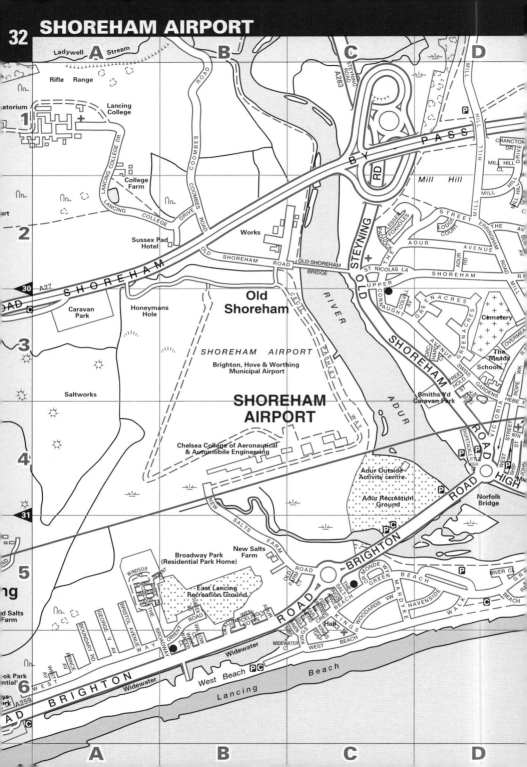

A Ladywell Stream **B** **C** STEYNING ROAD A283 **D**

Rifle Range

atorium

1 Lancing College

Lancing College DR

COOMBES ROAD

LANCING COLLEGE DRIVE

College Farm

COOMBES ROAD

BY PASS

RD

Mill Hill

CHANCTON DR

MILL HILL CL

MILL HILL

2 Court

Sussex Pad Hotel

OLD SHOREHAM ROAD

Works

OLD SHOREHAM ROAD

OLD SHOREHAM BRIDGE

STEYNING ROAD

ST NICOLAS LA

UPPER

CONNAUGHT

THE PADDOCK

LESSER FOXHOLES

LODGE COURT

STREET

ADUR

GREEN ACRES

GREENACRES

ADUR RD

SHOREHAM AVENUE

SHOREHAM

THE AV

ERINGHAM ROAD

MILL

RD

30 A27

SHOREHAM

ROAD

OLD SHOREHAM

RIVER

SHOREHAM

OVERMEAD

Cemetery

The Meads Schools

3 Caravan Park

Honeymans Hole

Old Shoreham

SHOREHAM AIRPORT

Brighton, Hove & Worthing Municipal Airport

CECIL

SLEY WAY

ADUR

Smiths Yd Caravan Park

ORCHARD VIEW

HARE LN

FREE HOLD

SWISS

GARDENS

ST

BIRCH CLOSE

HEBE RD

ROPE WK

Saltworks

SHOREHAM AIRPORT

VICTORIA ROAD

WEST STREET

NTH

JOHN ST

SHIP

4 Chelsea College of Aeronautical & Automobile Engineering

NEW SALTS FARM

Adur Outside Activity centre

HOPETACKLE

HIGH

HIGH ROAD

Norfolk Bridge

31

Adur Recreation Ground

BRIGHTON ROAD

P C

5 Broadway Park (Residential Park Home)

New Salts Farm

WINDSOR

East Lancing Recreation Ground

BRISTOL AVENUE

THE BROADWAY

GEORGE V AV

ORIENT

WILLOW

WEN

FARM ROAD

ADUR ROAD

WILLOW COTTS

Road

BEACH GREEN

MONDE WY

MARDYKE

WOODARDS VW

BEACH

WALK

HAVENSIDE

RIVER CL

BEACH

C

ng

d Salts Farm

BOUNDARY RD

PRINCE AV

WEST

GEORGE V AV

Widewater

WIDEWATER CT

KINGS BEACH

KINGS CRES

KINGS EXP

KINGS

WEST

Hall

KING STREET

6 ook Park ential

ys Park

BRIGHTON ROAD A259

WEST

Widewater

West Beach

P C

Lancing

Beach

Beach

A **B** **C** **D**